ANIMALS ARE AMAZING

# LIONS

BY VALERIE BODDEN

W

FRANKLIN WATTS
LONDON • SYDNEY

First published in the UK in 2012 by
Franklin Watts
338 Euston Road
London NW1 3BH

Franklin Watts Australia
Level 17/207 Kent Street
Sydney NSW 2000

First published by Creative Education,
an imprint of the Creative Company.
Copyright © 2010 Creative Education

ISBN 978 1 4451 1083 7
Dewey number: 599.7'57

A CIP catalogue record for this book
is available from the British Library.

Printed in China

Franklin Watts is a division of
Hachette Children's Books
an Hachette UK company
www.hachette.co.uk

Book and cover design by The Design Lab
Art direction by Rita Marshall

Photographs by Getty Images (John Giustina, Beverly
Joubert, Stan Osolinski, Panoramic Images, Valerie
Shaff, Anup Shah, Paul Souders, Art Wolfe, Norbert
Wu), iStockphoto (David T. Gomez, Eric Isselée)

# CONTENTS

# What are lions?

*Lions live in hot areas that have a lot of grass.*

**Lions** are big cats. They are the second-largest cat in the world. The only cat that grows bigger than the lion is the tiger. There are only two **species** of lion in the world.

**species** different types of the same animal.

# Lion facts

*This lion is showing off his deadly, sharp teeth!*

Lions have a strong body that is covered with fur. The fur can be yellow or brown. Male lions have a mane. A mane is the area of bushy hair around the lion's head and neck. Lions also have a long tail, big teeth and very sharp claws!

*A mane makes a male lion look even bigger.*

# Male and female lions

*Male lions are stronger, but females are faster.*

**Male** lions can grow to be 2.4 metres long. They can weigh more than two grown people! A female lion is a little smaller. She is called a lioness.

All lions can **roar**. It can be very loud. They roar to let other lions know where they are and to show how big and strong they are.

**roar** the loud, scary noise that a lion can make.

# Where lions live

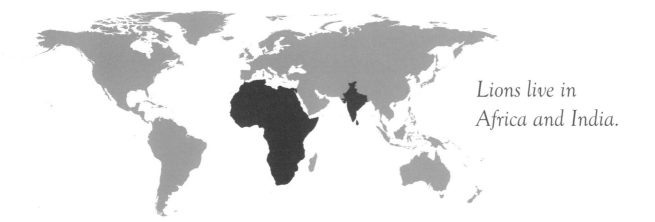

*Lions live in Africa and India.*

Most lions live on the **continent** of Africa. This is why they are called African lions. The area they live in is called the **savanna**. The other species of lion lives in India. They are called Asiatic (*ay-zhe-AT-ick*) lions. They live in a place called the Gir Forest.

**continent** one of Earth's seven big pieces of land.
**savanna** flat, hot land covered with grass and a few trees.

# Lion food

*A lion can eat 34 kg of meat in one meal.*

Lions are **carnivores**; they eat other animals. Some of their favourite animals to eat are zebras, wildebeest and antelopes. Sometimes lions eat elephants. A few lions have even eaten people!

**carnivore** an animal that only eats meat.

# New lions

*Female lions keep a careful watch over all the cubs.*

A mother lion gives birth to between two and six **cubs** at a time. At first, the cubs stay in a **den** with their mother. Cubs are born with their eyes shut. Their eyes open after about one week and they leave the den when they are five weeks old. They begin to learn how to hunt by playing with each other. Lions in the wild can live for 15 years.

**cubs**  baby lions.
**den**  a home that is hidden, like a cave.

# Pride life

Lions live in family groups called prides. Most prides have about 15 lions: one big male lion and lots of females and cubs. Prides also have one or two young male lions. They live with the pride until they are 2 or 3 years old. Then they leave and start prides of their own.

Adult lions spend a lot of time sleeping. About 20 hours each day! Cubs like to play and chase small animals.

*Lions like to rest during the hottest part of the day.*

# Hunting for food

*Lions often look for sick or old animals to catch and eat.*

**Lions** often hunt at night. They can sneak up on their **prey** more easily in the dark. But lions also hunt during the day. Female lions do most of the hunting. They usually work together as a team. They use their teeth and claws to kill their prey. The male lions get to eat first. The females and cubs have to wait until the males have finished eating.

**prey** an animal that is eaten by other animals.

# Lions and people

Today, people around the world can go to zoos to see lions. Some people watch lions perform in the circus. And some people even go to Africa to see lions in the wild. It is exciting to get close to these big cats!

*Zoo lions and wild lions like to spend time playing.*

# A lion story

**Why** do lions roar? People in Africa tell a story about this. They say that the lion used to sneak up on animals and eat them. One day, a **hare** put honey from a beehive on the lion while he slept. When the bees saw the honey, they stung the lion. The pain made the lion roar. From then on, the lion roared – and the animals always heard him coming!

**hare** an animal that looks like a rabbit but is bigger.

# Useful information

## Read More

*Leapfrog Learners: Big Cats* by Annabelle Lynch (Franklin Watts, 2012)

*Up Close: Big Cats* by Paul Harrison (Franklin Watts, 2011)

*Animal Instincts: A Fierce Lion* by Tom Jackson (Wayland, 2011)

## Websites

Enchanted Learning: Lions
*http://www.enchantedlearning.com/subjects/mammals/lion/coloring.shtml*
This site has lion facts and a picture to colour.

National Geographic Kids Creature Feature: Lions
*http://kids.nationalgeographic.com/Animals/CreatureFeature/Lion*
This site has lots of facts, pictures and videos of lions.

Every effort has been made by the Publishers to ensure that these websites are suitable for children, that they are of the highest educational value and that they contain no inappropriate or offensive material. However, because of the nature of the Internet, it is impossible to guarantee that the contents of these sites will not be altered. We strongly advise that Internet access is supervised by a responsible adult.

## Index